MY FEELINGS AND ME

T0343096

MY FEELINGS AND ME

An Hachette UK Company
www.hachette.co.uk

Vie Books, an imprint of Summersdale Publishers
Part of Octopus Publishing Group Limited
Carmelite House
50 Victoria Embankment
LONDON
EC4Y 0DZ
UK

www.summersdale.com

Printed and bound in Poland

ISBN: 978-1-80007-338-8

This FSC® label means that materials used for the product have been responsibly sourced

MIX
Paper | Supporting responsible forestry
FSC® C018236

Substantial discounts on bulk quantities of Summersdale books are available to corporations, professional associations and other organizations. For details contact general enquiries: telephone: +44 (0) 1243 771107 or email: enquiries@summersdale.com.

MY FEELINGS AND ME

A Child's Guide to Understanding Emotions

Poppy O'Neill

CONTENTS

FOREWORD

Amanda Ashman-Wymbs, Counsellor and Psychotherapist, registered and accredited by the British Association for Counselling and Psychotherapy

Having raised children and worked in schools and the private sector therapeutically for many years, it is clear to me that learning to manage and understand emotions is an area where children really need a lot of support. Often parents and other caring adults around them are not sure how to help them gain more emotional awareness and literacy.

My Feelings and Me by Poppy O'Neill is a great place for a child to start to understand the different feelings that they may be experiencing and learn how to talk about, accept and process these emotions in healthy and positive ways. Aimed at children aged 7–11, the handbook is packed with fun and friendly exercises and creative and calming activities that will help children to interact with their feelings in a safe and easily digestible way. The child is accompanied on their way by a friendly monster named Pop who's presence makes this book an attractive space to explore their feelings and also be introduced to other areas of emotional intelligence such as body awareness, the connection between thinking and feeling, empathy, basic neuroscience, as well as the importance of growing in gratitude and taking care of your body.

I highly recommend this valuable and much needed book as a great resource for helping children to manage and understand feelings.

INTRODUCTION: A GUIDE FOR PARENTS AND CARERS

My Feelings and Me presents practical activities and ideas, based on techniques used by child psychologists, to help your child develop the skills to understand their own emotions and how they affect them, as well as the emotions of others. This will support them to build resilience, confidence and empathy.

Your child will be encouraged to think about how they feel, and how their full range of emotions affect their thoughts and actions. They'll be guided through practical tips on how to calm big emotions, as well as how to express them safely and respectfully.

Perhaps your child is confused by their feelings or seems to struggle with overwhelming emotional reactions. Maybe they seem to keep everything inside and lack an outlet for expressing themselves. The thing about emotions is everyone has them, so the key is learning how to feel comfortable and accepting toward whatever feelings arise.

This book is aimed at children aged 7–11, an age when many still need guidance in soothing big emotions that might also make them feel self-conscious, as it's also a time when their social awareness increases. Coupled with the onset of puberty and all the new feelings that brings, it can be a turbulent and confusing time, emotionally, for everyone. If that sounds familiar, you're not alone. With your support and guidance, they can become more comfortable with their feelings, respectful of others' and resilient in the face of challenges.

Talking to your child about feelings

Discussing feelings with your child is the simplest way to begin understanding them better, but it can be difficult to know where to start! Here's an easy-to-remember acronym that will help you:

P Playfulness: approach the subject with light-heartedness – don't take it too seriously.

A Acceptance: accept whatever feelings your child talks about. Feelings are not right or wrong – they just are.

C Curiosity: show an interest in their emotions and ideas – ask your child what it's like to be them.

E Empathy: show that you understand their feelings, and will comfort and stay with them.

Remember: talking about emotions is not going to be a one-off conversation; it's more like a habit to form. You don't need to solve any problems or come up with any definite answers in a single chat. Sharing emotions with someone you trust is one of the best ways to soothe and move on from difficult experiences, so the simple act of talking is, in many cases, enough.

> **Developed by psychotherapist Dr Daniel Hughes as a way of connecting with others, PACE creates safe, productive conversations and relationships. It's backed up by neuroscience, and used by therapists and psychologists all over the world.**

MY FEELINGS AND ME

How to use this book: For parents and carers

This book is for your child, so it's best to follow their lead in terms of how involved you'll be. Some children will be happy to make their way through the activities by themselves, while others might need a little guidance and encouragement.

Even if your child wants to do the activities independently, it's a good idea to show an interest and talk about the book. Ask about what they've learned or realized, as well as checking whether there are any parts they've found helpful, interesting or challenging. One way to spark a conversation about feelings is to ask how this book has made your child feel!

The activities are designed to get your child thinking about the way their emotions and minds work, so it's important to reassure them that there are no wrong answers and that they can go at their own pace. Hopefully, this book will help your child to understand a bit better how emotions work and feel more comfortable expressing them. However, if you have any serious concerns about your child's mental health, your doctor is the best person to go to for further advice.

HOW TO USE THIS BOOK: A GUIDE FOR CHILDREN

Do your emotions sometimes seem confusing or upsetting? It's very normal to feel this way! Here are some examples of what it means to find feelings tricky:

- You find it difficult to talk about feelings

- You try to keep your feelings hidden from others

- When your feelings are hurt, you pretend to be fine

- When you have a big emotion, you find it hard to control your actions

- You feel worried or scared when other people are feeling big emotions

If that sounds like you sometimes, or all of the time, this book is here to help – you will learn all about emotions and how to express them in a way that's comfortable for you. Everyone struggles with their feelings sometimes; they just have different ways of showing them on the outside.

In these pages you'll find lots of activities and ideas, which you can read through at your own pace. You can ask for help from your grown-up at any point, and there might be things in here that you'd like to talk to them about, too. This book is for you and about you, so there are no wrong answers – you're the expert!

INTRODUCING
POP THE MONSTER

Hi! It's so good to meet you. I'm Pop and I'm here to guide you
through this book. Do you ever feel curious about your feelings?
I do – they're so interesting. There are lots of fun activities and ideas
to help you learn in this book. Are you ready? Let's get started.

PART 1: MY EMOTIONS AND ME

In this chapter we're going to learn a bit about you and about feelings. Getting to know yourself and your emotions is a really important part of understanding them.

ACTIVITY: ALL ABOUT ME

First, let's learn a bit about you!

My name is...

I am __ years old.

I live with...

My favourite thing to do is...

Three words that describe me are...

ACTIVITY: MY FEELINGS

Every day, we have lots of different feelings. When do these emotions come up for you?

I feel happy when..._____
_____.

I feel sad when..._____
_____.

I feel calm when..._____
_____.

I feel angry when..._____
_____.

I feel shy when..._____
_____.

I feel worried when..._____
_____.

I feel brave when..._____
_____.

I feel disgusted when..._____
_____.

WHAT ARE EMOTIONS?

Emotions are things we feel in our body and mind in response to what happens around us and the thoughts we have. It's not just human beings that have emotions – animals have them, too.

They help you to learn how to stay safe from danger – like when you feel scared of a busy road – and how to recognize when something is good for you, like when you feel happy playing with your friends. Other emotions tell you when to ask for help – like when you feel sad and need a hug – or show you when someone isn't treating you well, like feeling angry when someone calls you a rude name.

In the same way a runny nose helps to get all the germs out of your body when you're ill, emotions help you to understand and learn from what happens to you, so you don't get stuck feeling down for longer than you need to.

The four basic emotions are: happiness, sadness, fear and anger. There are loads of other feelings, but they're all linked to one of these main ones.

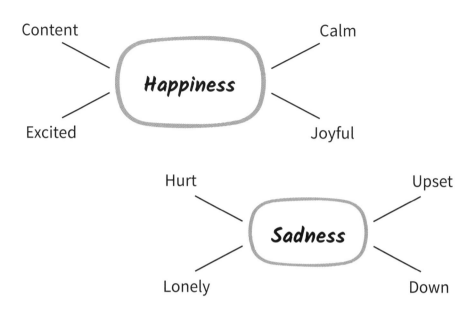

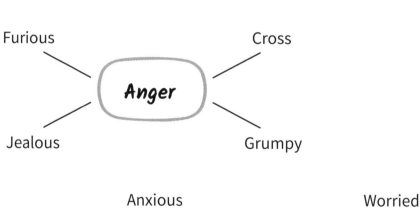

I AM
SPECIAL

ACTIVITY: LISTEN TO YOUR THOUGHTS

Take a moment to listen to the thoughts buzzing around in your head right now. Write a few of them down here:

Emotions and thoughts both start in the brain, so they're closely linked. If you feel happy, your thoughts will be happy, and if you feel angry, your thoughts will match, too.

ALL EMOTIONS ARE OK

Did you know that all emotions are good ones? It's true! While some of them don't feel very nice when you're feeling them, that doesn't mean that they're bad or wrong, or that they can hurt you.

Everyone is feeling emotions all day long. Mostly, they change quite quickly, but sometimes they hang around all day. Not every emotion gets shown on the outside, so we don't ever really know how people are feeling, unless we know them really well and talk to them a lot.

Sometimes you might feel embarrassed about your emotions or think that you're feeling the wrong ones. It's OK to feel whatever you feel, and just because you can't always explain your emotions, it doesn't mean that they are any less important.

ACTIVITY: A WHOLE RAINBOW OF FEELINGS

Experiencing all kinds of feelings is what makes life interesting. Sometimes you feel lots of emotions at once, and sometimes one at a time. Other times it's hard to tell what you're feeling, but your rainbow of feelings is always a part of you.

Can you colour in the rainbow?

ACTIVITY: MATCH THE FEELINGS TO THE FACES

How can you tell how someone is feeling? The first place to look for clues is on their face! That's where we show our emotions, and we're pretty good at spotting even small signs. Can you match the faces to the emotions? Draw a line to connect them up.

Angry

Surprised

Disgusted

Calm

Excited

Worried

Happy

Sad

Did you know? Babies learn to tell the difference between the emotions their parents show from as young as four months old.

EVERYBODY FEELS SAD SOMETIMES

PART 2: EXPRESSING YOUR FEELINGS

Showing how you feel is really important… but it can also be really tricky! In this chapter you're going to find out how you can let your feelings out.

WHY TALKING ABOUT FEELINGS HELPS

When you're feeling really big emotions, a part of your brain – right in the middle – called the amygdala is in charge. It's often called your "feeling brain" and is about the size of an almond.

Putting how you're feeling into words helps the "thinking brain" (which is in charge of words, memories and knowledge, and can be found at the top and front of your brain) take over, so your feeling brain becomes a little calmer.

The more you talk about your feelings, the more your feeling brain can connect with your thinking brain. So even if something really bad or scary happened to you, if you talk about it, over time those feelings will feel easier and smaller.

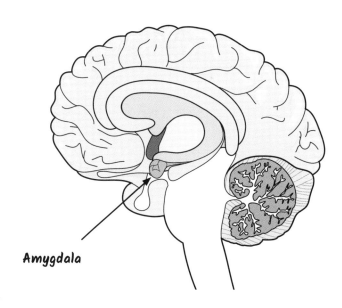

Amygdala

HOW WOULD YOU FEEL...

The things we find easy and hard are different for everybody. Write about how these things make you feel – or draw emoji faces:

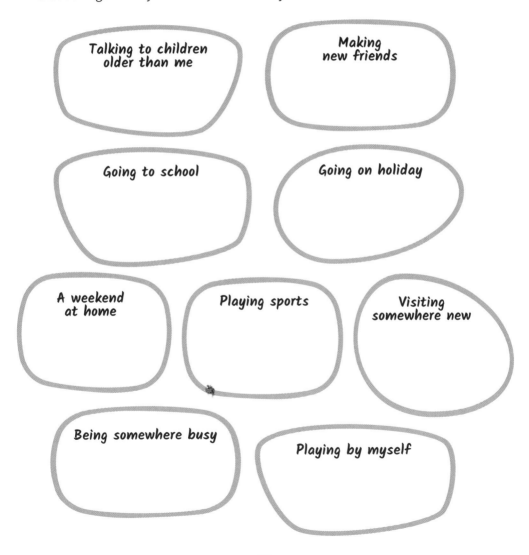

Talking to children older than me

Making new friends

Going to school

Going on holiday

A weekend at home

Playing sports

Visiting somewhere new

Being somewhere busy

Playing by myself

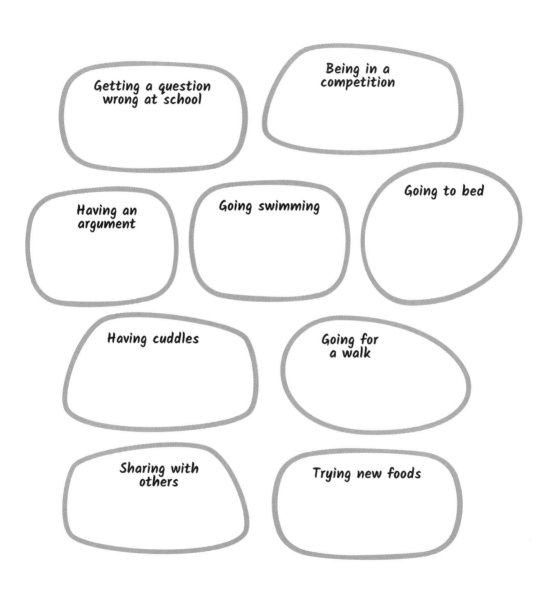

Getting a question wrong at school

Being in a competition

Having an argument

Going swimming

Going to bed

Having cuddles

Going for a walk

Sharing with others

Trying new foods

LISTEN TO YOUR BODY

Your body is the best place to look for clues about your emotions. It's helpful to have a name for what you're feeling, but sometimes that doesn't happen, and that's OK! It doesn't make your emotion any more or less real.

Sometimes emotions show up as a tummy ache, a heavy feeling or a big rush of energy.

Take a moment to listen to your body. You don't need to give a name to anything you can feel – just notice what you find.

ACTIVITY: HOW DO YOU FEEL RIGHT NOW?

Let's take some time to think a little more about how you're feeling right now.

First, your emotions – you can circle the words that come closest to how you feel, write your own or draw:

Disgusted   **Thoughtful**

                    Sad   **Calm**

    Angry   **Nervous**

Worried   **Confused**

                                Happy

                    Excited

Do you know why you might be feeling this way?

For example: *I feel worried because I'm meeting my new teacher tomorrow.*

_____

_____

_____

_____

_____

Can you feel any other sensations? Circle the words or write your own:

Warm
    Achy
    Tired

Itchy
    Thirsty

Hungry

Cold
    Comfortable

Think again about your emotions. Where can you feel them? Draw shapes on this picture to show where, and how, it feels in your body:

I feel worry as an aching tummy

ACTIVITY: MOOD TRACKER

Now you're getting used to checking how you're feeling, you can keep track using a mood tracker.

Pick a colour for each emotion, then colour each square to show how you mostly felt that day.

Happy	**Upset**
Bored	**Sad**
Calm	**Excited**
Angry	**Worried**

MOOD TRACKER

Mon	Tue	Wed	Thu	Fri	Sat	Sun

I CAN
BOUNCE BACK

ACTIVITY: DRAW YOUR FEELINGS

Sometimes it's not easy to put feelings into words. That's why you can also express emotions by drawing, playing and moving your body. Use this page to show your emotions by using colours, patterns and pictures.

You can scribble, doodle and draw anything you like – animals, people, things, places, plants… They don't need to look like they do in real life and your images don't need to make sense. Let your feelings guide you and have fun!

Can you fill up the whole page with drawing?

YOU ARE NOT ALONE

Emotions can make you feel lonely sometimes, especially when it seems like everyone else is having different or smaller ones.

Everyone feels big emotions sometimes. You can have all kinds of feelings – there's nothing wrong with you for the things you feel – and emotions can't harm you.

By reading this book and thinking about your emotions, you're doing a really brave thing that will help you to express yourself. When you talk about your feelings with someone you trust, you will feel better and realize that you are not alone.

HOW TO TALK ABOUT FEELINGS

Talking about feelings can be tricky and even a bit frightening! Here are some clever tips to help make it easier:

- ❀ Talk about how you feel – not how you think other people are feeling

- ❀ Take a deep breath if something feels difficult to say

- ❀ Write down what you'd like to say

- ❀ Talk while doing something else (like walking, baking or playing a game)

- ❀ Say how talking is making you feel

- ❀ Stop if you need a break

- ❀ Use drawing to show how you're feeling

- ❀ Move your body to show how you're feeling

- ❀ Use characters from books and TV shows to show how you're feeling

- ❀ Be playful – even if you're talking about a difficult emotion, you can still be creative, if that feels right

ACTIVITY: PEOPLE I CAN TALK TO

Who can you talk to about feelings? Not everybody is a good fit, and that's OK!
If you can think of one or two people, that's plenty.

I can talk about feelings with...	I feel comfortable talking to them because...

ACTIVITY: I CAN TALK ABOUT MY FEELINGS

Is there something you'd like to talk about, but it's hard? If not, that's OK. You can come back to this page when something's troubling you and you want to make a plan.

Use the things we've learned so far to finish the sentences.

I wish I could talk about…

_____

_____

_____

_____

_____

I can talk to…

_____

_____

_____

_____

_____

Something that could make it feel easier is…

_____

_____

_____

_____

_____

POP ASKS FOR HELP

Asking for help is hard! Big emotions can make it even harder.

Pop is writing a story and gets stuck. Pop starts to feel angry and frustrated. Pop wants to rip up the story and throw it in the bin!

Pop was really brave to ask for help instead of ripping up the story.

WHY IT'S OK TO FEEL NEGATIVE EMOTIONS

Some people think that we shouldn't show emotions like anger or fear on the outside, because it makes others feel uncomfortable. But if you keep your feelings all on the inside, they get crowded and stuck.

The tricky thing about negative emotions like anger, sadness and worry is that they can sometimes make us want to behave in ways that upset or hurt others.

Learning how to express negative emotions in ways that keep us and others safe is always OK and a brilliant skill. Keep reading to learn more!

When you're feeling a big emotion, your body might want to:

❀ Hit   ❀ Run away   ❀ Curl up small

❀ Kick   ❀ Hide

❀ Throw things   ❀ Shout

Can you think of any others?

_____

_____

_____

_____

_____

_____

These urges are your body's way of trying to let the big emotion out, but often it's not safe to do these things, because you could hurt yourself or someone else.

So how can you help your body to let out big emotions safely? Here are some ideas:

- 🦋 Jump on a trampoline
- 🦋 Stomp on the ground
- 🦋 Hit a cushion
- 🦋 Drum on the floor
- 🦋 Drum on your knees
- 🦋 Sit somewhere safe and quiet

- 🦋 Cry (it's always OK to cry!)
- 🦋 Give yourself a big hug
- 🦋 Hug someone
- 🦋 Write down your thoughts
- 🦋 Say what you're feeling

Can you think of any others?

_____

_____

_____

_____

_____

_____

_____

_____

_____

CALMING WORDS FOR WHEN YOU'RE WORRIED

Worry can make your thoughts go round and round. Once you start worrying, it's difficult to stop!

Saying, thinking or writing down calming words can help you to feel better. Try these ones next time you feel worried.

Everything is going to be OK

I can take a deep breath

I am safe

I can ask for help

I can say no

It's OK to make mistakes

ACTIVITY: TRIANGLE BREATHING

Concentrating on your breathing is a brilliant way to calm big emotions like worry or anger. Trace your finger along the sides of this triangle, counting to three each time, as you breathe.

When you feel big emotions, your breathing gets quick and shallow. By spending a bit of time to take deep breaths, your body can start to feel calm again.

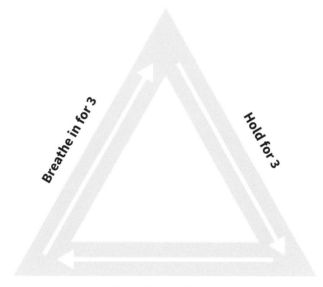

Breathe in for 3

Hold for 3

Breathe out for 3

ACTIVITY: I LIKE MYSELF

Feelings are a big part of what makes you special. But you are more than just feelings! Your likes and dislikes, the way you treat others, and the choices you make all mix together to make your personality.

Write or draw in the thought bubbles:

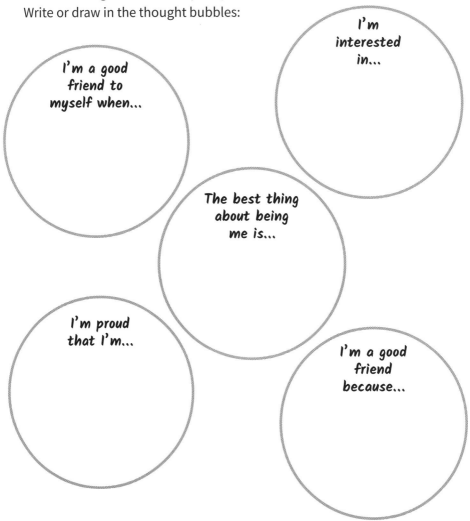

I'm a good
friend to
myself when...

I'm
interested
in...

The best thing
about being
me is...

I'm proud
that I'm...

I'm a good
friend
because...

Can you draw a picture of yourself in the frame? Try sitting in front of a mirror, so you can get a really good look at your face!

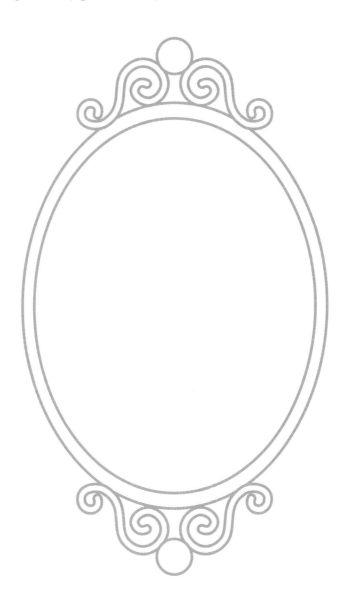

I LIKE MYSELF!

PART 3: UNDERSTANDING YOUR FEELINGS

In this chapter you will learn more about how emotions work and spend time discovering what it feels like to be you.

THOUGHTS, FEELINGS AND ACTIONS

Thoughts and feelings work together. If they match, the feeling gets bigger and the thoughts get faster!

Pop's feeling excited about a trip to the big city. Pop's thinking about all the things that'll happen there, so the excited feeling grows and the excited thoughts race.

The way we're thinking and feeling shows on the outside through our actions.

So if Pop's feeling excited and thinking excited thoughts to match, Pop might be running around, talking about the trip and asking lots of questions about it.

Sometimes, an excited feeling can turn into worried feelings, thoughts and actions, like thinking and talking about all the things that might go wrong!

Later that day, Pop's still feeling excited, but Pop starts to think: "I can be patient and excited. I can enjoy today and look forward to the trip." So Pop's excited feeling is still there, but it's smaller, calmer and easier to feel.

It's not always easy to think like this! It's OK to need practice and help from a grown-up to calm big feelings.

How might Pop act if Pop's thinking calming thoughts? Circle the answers below, as many as you think – you can add some of your own, too!

Talking about feelings

Reading a book

Playing outside

Drawing a picture

Making a list of things to bring on the trip

Packing a rucksack for the trip

Taking deep breaths

Talking about something else

Surprise! All of these answers are correct. It's OK to feel big feelings and show them on the outside. It's also OK to take a break from them, by doing things that calm your body and mind – and these are different for everyone.

ACTIVITY: GET TO KNOW YOUR FEELINGS, THOUGHTS AND ACTIONS

When Pop feels **sad**, it feels like ***a heavy heart***, and Pop **asks for lots of hugs**.
How does it feel to be you, and how do you show your feelings on the outside? Fill in the gaps here:

When I feel excited, it feels like _____ and I _____.

When I feel sad, it feels like _____ and I _____.

When I feel worried, it feels like _____ and I _____.

When I feel happy, it feels like _____ and I _____.

When I feel angry, it feels like _____ and I _____.

When I feel embarrassed, it feels like _____ and I _____.

WHAT IS SELF-TALK?

Self-talk means the way we think about ourselves. It's the voice you use to talk to yourself in your mind, and also the way you talk about yourself with other people.

If you use positive self-talk, that means you're kind to yourself: you talk to and about yourself like a good friend – even when you're having a hard time or feeling big feelings. Positive self-talk sounds like…

"It's OK to feel sad"

"I'm trying my best"

"Well done me!"

If you have negative self-talk, the voice in your mind is unkind and makes you feel even worse when you're having a tough day. Negative self-talk sounds like…

"You look silly"

"You need to try harder"

"Stop crying"

Everyone has a mix of both positive and negative self-talk. The hardest time to be kind to yourself can be when you're feeling big feelings, but that's also the most important.

Speaking to yourself kindly when you're feeling big emotions makes them feel easier and helps to calm your body. Keep reading to learn how!

ACTIVITY: GET TO KNOW YOUR SELF-TALK VOICE

Take a moment to close your eyes and listen to your thoughts. Some of them might be about other things, but listen closely and you'll hear your self-talk voice.

It's the voice that describes you, imagines what other people think or feel, and predicts what's going to happen in the future.

Can you hear your self-talk voice? What kind of face might it have, if it were a person? Circle the one that feels right, or you can draw your own.

Your self-talk voice will probably change, depending on how you're feeling. Come back to this page when you're feeling really good about yourself and jot down some of the words that your self-talk voice uses:

_____

_____

_____

Another time, when you're feeling down, worried or angry, come back to this page and write down what your self-talk voice says:

_____

_____

_____

THOUGHTS ARE NOT FACTS

Thoughts come from your brain. That doesn't mean that none of them are true – most of them are based on things that have happened to us before, mixed with the emotions we're feeling.

Thoughts are your brain's way of trying to make sense of the world. When there's something you're not sure about, your brain will do its best to make up a story to explain it.

For example, a group of kids you don't know are at the park. You walk past them and they all laugh. You don't know why they laughed, so your brain might make up one of these stories:

🦋 They're laughing at me

🦋 One of them just told a funny joke

🦋 They want to make me feel embarrassed

🦋 They're just having a nice time at the park – they have no reason to laugh at me

Now, these things can't *all* be true. The story your brain makes up is usually more to do with how you feel about yourself than what has actually happened. Can you choose one of the kinder stories?

It's OK if your brain usually comes up with quite negative thoughts and stories. Try to remember that thoughts are not facts and see if you can pick a more positive one.

The brain makes up negative stories in lots of different ways – these are called "thinking errors".

Here are the main types of thinking errors and what they sound like:

❀ All-or-nothing thinking: if something isn't perfect, I've failed completely

❀ Over-generalizing: if one thing goes wrong, everything will go wrong

❀ Focus on the negatives: if one thing goes wrong, that's the only thing I can think about – even if other things go right

❀ Fortune-telling: I know I'll fail

❀ Mind-reading: I know everyone thinks badly of me

❀ Catastrophic thinking: everything is going to be ruined

❀ Feelings are facts: I feel ugly, so I must be ugly

❀ Magnified thinking: the things I don't like about myself are the most important ones about me; the things I like about myself aren't important

❀ Negative comparison: other people are better than me in every way

❀ Unrealistic expectations: I should be perfect at everything on my first try

❀ Putting yourself down: I'm a failure

❀ Blaming yourself: it's my fault when things go wrong

❀ Blaming others: I would do better if everyone else was nicer to me

Do any of these sound like your self-talk voice? Draw a circle around any that you recognize.

ACTIVITY: FLIP YOUR THOUGHTS!

So, we've learned that thoughts aren't facts, and that the thoughts we have can make a difference to the emotions we feel, and vice versa. The next step is to learn how to choose a kind, hopeful or positive thought over one that makes you feel worse.

This is called flipping your thoughts.

Pop has been invited to a birthday party. Pop's painted a picture to give as a birthday present – Pop feels nervous about giving the present!

Hold on, that sounds like a thinking error! What's Pop's brain up to? It's fortune-telling. Pop can't know what will happen next, so Pop's brain is making up a story.

Pop remembers that thoughts are not facts and chooses a more hopeful thought instead.

Now you try! Draw an arrow from each negative thought to its matching positive one to see if you can flip it.

Negative thought		Positive thought
No one at school likes me		I have good friends
This maths problem is too hard – I can't do it		I can ask for help
Everyone will laugh at my new glasses		I can't wait to see if my friends spot my new glasses

Can you come up with some more kind, hopeful and positive thoughts to flip your own negative ones?

Negative thought		Positive thought

Each time a thought tries to get you down, write it here and see if you can flip it into a kinder and more hopeful thought.

ACTIVITY: PICK AND MIX!

Pick a sweet from each jar to make a feel-good sentence!

Write your feel-good sentences here:

WHAT YOU CAN AND CAN'T CONTROL

When you're feeling worried, it can seem like you need to fix things or solve a problem. But a lot of the time, what makes us worry are things we can't change or control.

I can control:
The way I treat others
My words
My actions
My choices
Who I am friends with
My effort

I can't control:
How other people treat me
Other people's actions
Other people's words
Who is in my family
The weather
Getting ill

Thinking about what you can and can't control will help you to feel calmer. This works by reminding the brain that it's not its job to know the future or take responsibility for other people's actions. Flip back to this page next time you feel worried.

I AM LEARNING AND GROWING EVERY DAY

THE WORRY MOUNTAIN

Feeling worried is a bit like climbing a mountain.

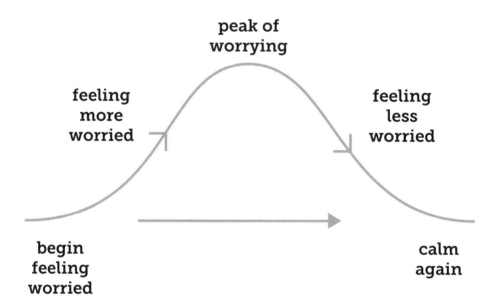

peak of worrying

feeling more worried

feeling less worried

begin feeling worried

calm again

If you start to feel worry building inside you, imagine a mountain and at the top is where you feel most worried. Once you reach that point, you know that your worried feeling won't last for too much longer, and you will start to feel calmer and calmer until the worry has gone.

ACTIVITY: THROW AWAY YOUR WORRIED THOUGHTS

It's difficult to get rid of worried thoughts – they buzz around in your head and won't go away!

Here's a clever trick that can help to let worried thoughts out of your mind.

Write them here, then cut out the squares and throw your worries in the recycling bin! Be careful cutting out your worries!

ACTIVITY: GET PLENTY OF EXERCISE

Being active is super important for keeping your body healthy, but did you know it keeps your brain healthy too? Exercising and moving your body releases special feel-good chemicals in your brain, helping you feel happier and more confident. Can you draw yourself doing your favourite kind of exercise? (It doesn't need to be a sport – dancing, running around with your friends and climbing trees are all excellent exercise too!)

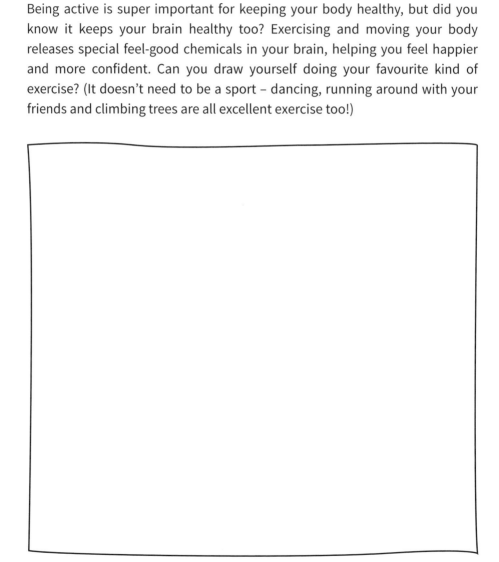

CALMING-DOWN TRICKS

When you're feeling a big emotion, it's hard to think of ways to calm down! That's why it's a good idea to try out plenty of calming-down tricks, so you'll know what works for you and what doesn't.

You can come back to this book any time you're struggling with how you're feeling. It will remind you of ways you can help the emotion move through and out of your body.

On the next few pages there are loads of ideas for cooling big emotions. Try them out, and if some of them don't fit, that's OK!

PAUSE TO RESET

Can you press pause on your emotions? Not really. But you can press pause on your thoughts and actions.

Pausing means stopping what you're doing, taking a big, deep breath and having a break from whatever you're thinking about.

Try it now – press the big pause button and count to three.

Did pressing pause help you to feel calmer?

BREATHING EXERCISES

Concentrating on the way you breathe in and out is a wonderful way to calm big emotions. Try these fun animal breathing exercises – which is your favourite?

Snake breathing

🦋 Breathe in through your nose to the count of three.

🦋 Breathe out through your mouth, making a hissing noise like a snake.

🦋 Do this three times.

Lion breathing

❀ Sit on the ground and lean forward, so your hands are flat on the floor, and your arms are strong and straight.

❀ Breathe in through your nose to the count of three.

❀ Breathe out through your wide-open mouth, with your tongue sticking out, like a roaring lion.

❀ Do this three times.

Bee breathing

❀ Breathe in through your nose to the count of three.

❀ As you breathe out through your mouth, make a buzzing bee sound, with your teeth pressed together.

❀ Do this three times.

GROUNDING YOURSELF

Imagine you are a tree. Your branches reach up and are moved by a gentle breeze. Your trunk stands tall. Think about strong roots growing from the soles of your feet down into the ground. Feel how the earth supports you.

Can you add roots to this picture?

Thinking about how you are connected to planet Earth is a great way to calm big emotions. It works because it takes your focus away from what you are feeling and onto the world around you.

WHAT IS MINDFULNESS?

Mindfulness means being aware and paying attention to all your senses. When you are mindful, thoughts and feelings become calmer, because you are focusing on what is happening in the present moment.

You can do almost anything mindfully! Here's how to be mindful at the park:

- 🦋 Walk slowly and notice the trees and plants around you

- 🦋 Breathe deeply – what does the park smell like?

- 🦋 Touch the grass, the bark of a tree, the chain on the swings

- 🦋 Choose a branch or a patch of grass and look closely at it – what do you see?

Try it next time you go to the park! Keep reading for more ways to be mindful.

ACTIVITY: MINDFUL COLOURING

Colouring is a very mindful activity, because you concentrate on how your pencil is moving and the marks it makes. Colour this picture and see if you feel calmer.

ACTIVITY: MINDFULNESS ROCKS!

Do you have a collection of small rocks or stones? Beads or Lego bricks work just as well! Trace the patterns on the opposite page onto a piece of paper, then lay it flat and take your time arranging your rocks, beads or bricks along the lines.

Using small objects to make patterns helps to calm your mind because you are concentrating on what you are doing with your hands, rather than on your thoughts or feelings. Can you come up with any more ideas for patterns of your own?

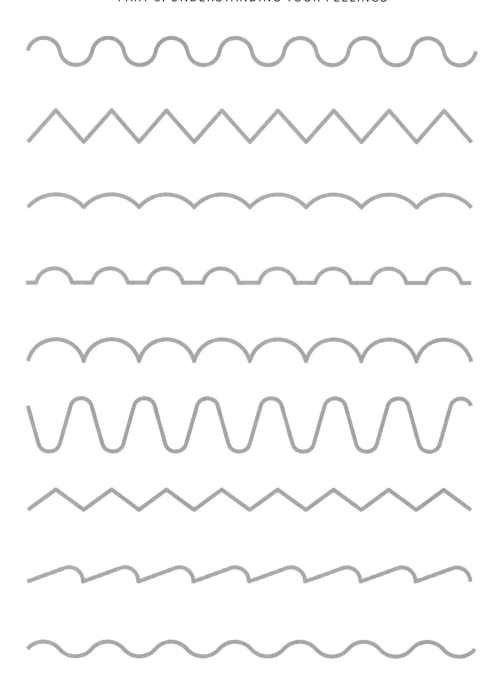

ACTIVITY: MINDFUL MEDITATION

Meditating helps your whole body and mind to feel calm. Try it before you go to sleep or when you're feeling full of worries.

Here's how…

1. Sit or lie down somewhere quiet and comfortable, and close your eyes. You might like to set a timer for one minute or play a relaxing song.

2. Imagine a bead on a piece of string. Imagine you are holding one end of the string in each hand, and the bead is at the centre. Concentrate on the bead – what colour is it? Does it have a pattern?

3. If you start thinking of something else, the bead slides down to one end of the string. It's OK if this happens, and it will definitely happen! If the bead slides, just imagine it back to the middle of the string.

4. When the timer rings or the song finishes, your meditation is complete.

ACTIVITY: MY FEELINGS CARDS

Cut out these conversation cards to help talk about feelings. Shuffle the cards and ask a friend or family member to pick one. The questions are for everyone to answer!

How do you feel right now?	**What's something or someone you miss?**
What's something you're looking forward to?	**What's something that annoys you?**
What does it mean to be a good friend?	**Have you felt upset today?**

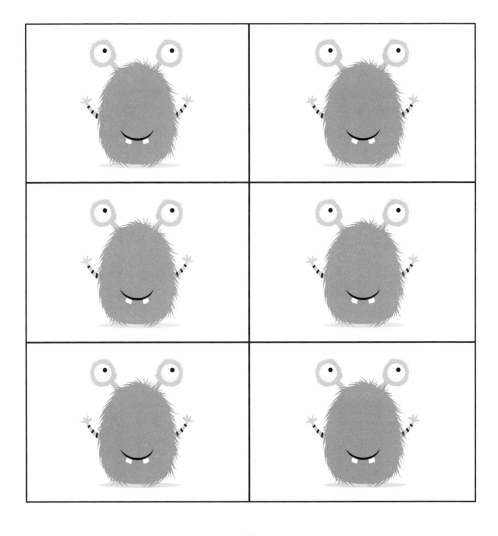

I CAN DO
HARD THINGS

PART 4:
ALL ABOUT EMPATHY

Empathy is a feelings superpower! In this chapter we're going to learn all about what empathy is and how it works.

WHAT IS EMPATHY?

Empathy is the ability to understand what another person is feeling. Without empathy, it's very difficult to have friendships or even talk to other people. The good news is, we begin learning how to empathize when we're babies, so you're already doing it without noticing!

If you can imagine how another person feels, you can work out how to be kind to them, be a good friend and work together to solve problems.

ACTIVITY: IN THEIR SHOES

Take a look at the names of the emotions in the bubbles below and on the next page. Think about all the things that someone who is feeling each one of them might say, think and do. Write down your ideas around the bubbles.

Example: I'm so lucky

Happy

Example: Breathing more quickly

Angry

Example: Asking for a hug

_____
_____
_____

_____
_____
_____

Sad

_____
_____
_____

_____
_____
_____

_____
_____
_____

Example: What if I fall?

_____
_____
_____

_____
_____
_____

Worried

_____
_____
_____

_____
_____
_____

_____
_____
_____

I AM
KIND

EVERYONE IS DIFFERENT!

Empathy is a superpower because everyone is different. The way we can imagine how others are feeling is an amazing skill, and it's OK to make mistakes. Some people are very good at hiding how they feel inside, and emotions can look different on different people.

For example, when Pop feels happy, Pop is smiley and quiet. When Fizz feels happy, Fizz wants to sing and dance.

So you can use your empathy superpower to guess how someone is feeling and how you can show kindness, but everyone is the expert on how they feel inside themselves.

ACTIVITY: UNDERSTANDING EMOTIONS

Read the mini stories – how do you think Pop is feeling? Write down your ideas.

Pop is playing football with friends. Pop has a chance to score a goal but might miss.

Pop might feel…_____

_____

_____

It's lunchtime and Pop wants to sit with three friends. But there are no spare seats next to Pop's friends.

Pop might feel…_____

_____

_____

Pop tried really hard this term and gets a reading award in front of the whole school.

Pop might feel…_____

_____

_____

Pop's new water bottle has gone missing. Pop thinks someone has stolen it.

Pop might feel…_____

_____

_____

ACTIVITY: WHEN SOMEONE ELSE IS FEELING BIG FEELINGS

How does it feel when you're close to someone who is feeling big or tricky emotions like anger or sadness?

Colour in the feelings and sensations you feel.

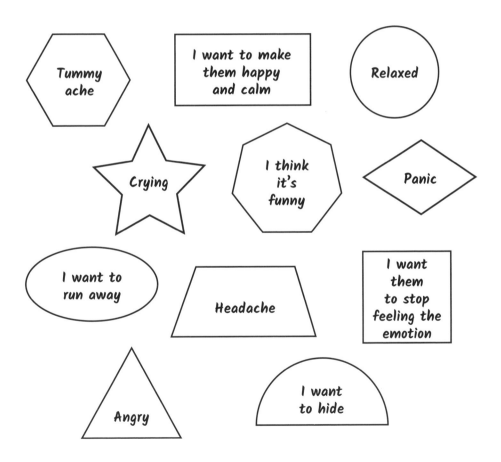

All kinds of feelings happen when we're with other people. Sometimes we start to feel the same as those around us or worry about their feelings. Sometimes we want to comfort them and other times we want to move away.

However you feel around another person is OK, and it's important to know that it's never your job to change someone else's emotions.

Everyone's feelings are their own. We can show each other kindness and empathy, and look after our own feelings at the same time.

My feelings are mine

If other people's emotions make you feel upset or worried, try this special trick.

Imagine a bubble around you, and inside it's safe and quiet. Your feelings are inside the bubble, and everyone else's are outside it. Take three deep breaths.

You can take your feelings bubble with you wherever you go. Your feelings bubble doesn't stop you from showing kindness to other people – in fact, it helps you to be an even better friend!

BECOME AN EXPERT LISTENER

Listening is a brilliant way to show empathy. When you listen carefully to another person, they know that they matter and that you care about how they feel.

Here's how to be a great listener:

- ❦ Look – keep your eyes on the person speaking.

- ❦ Move – smile, nod and turn toward the person to show that you understand.

- ❦ Be patient – it's OK if you disagree or have an idea, but wait until they've finished before you speak.

- ❦ Ask questions – to show that you're interested and want to understand.

- ❦ Respect – other people might feel and think differently to you and it's OK if your opinions don't match; it doesn't mean either of you is wrong.

You also deserve to be listened to! Who do you know that's a great listener?

ACTIVITY: SPREAD POSITIVITY

When you're feeling great, you can give a boost of positivity to someone else! Giving compliments is an easy way of spreading happiness.

Colour in and cut out these compliment cards – you could stick them around your neighbourhood, leave one in a library book, send one through the post or give them out to your friends and family. Write your own compliments on the blank cards.

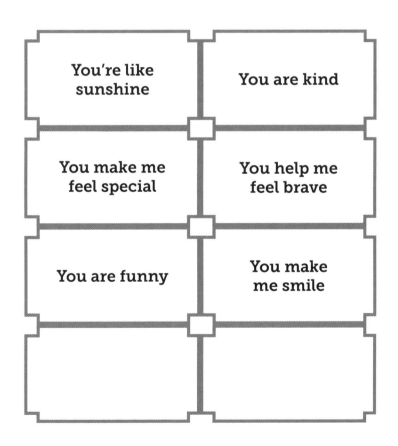

ACTIVITY: SEEING THE OTHER SIDE

There is always more than one way of looking at something. Considering how other people might think and feel is the key to empathy. It's OK to disagree with each other, and hearing different points of view helps us all to learn and grow.

For each idea, write your opinion and think of at least one other one that someone else might have.

Idea	My opinion	Another opinion
Best food		
Favourite season		
Best movie		
Favourite colour		
Cutest animal		

ACTIVITY: MAKE A STORY WITH A FRIEND

Being creative together is a wonderful way to get to know another person and explore feelings. Ask a friend or family member to play this story-making game with you. All you need is a pencil or pen each.

Take turns writing the next sentence of the story. You can keep going on a piece of scrap paper if you run out of space!

I was eating my lunch and you'll never guess what happened… _____

_____

_____

_____

_____

_____

_____

_____

_____

_____

_____

_____

_____

_____

_____

_____

_____

_____

_____

_____

_____
_____
_____
_____
_____
_____
_____
_____
_____
_____
_____
_____
_____
_____
_____
_____
_____
_____
_____
_____
_____
_____
_____
_____
_____
_____
_____
_____
_____
_____
_____
_____

STANDING UP FOR YOURSELF

Sometimes when we stand up for ourselves and look after our own feelings, other people don't like it. That's what makes it so difficult, but it doesn't mean that you've done something wrong!

A lot of the time, standing up for yourself takes bravery. Practising ways to do it with some added kindness can help you to feel even braver.

If you stand up for yourself with kindness and the other person is unkind to you, you don't have to do what they say. You can say "no" or "stop" really firmly. If someone is hurting you, or doing something that makes you feel uncomfortable or afraid, you don't have to be kind.

ACTIVITY: HELP POP THE MONSTER FEEL BETTER

Pop's going on holiday next week and is feeling full of worries! Pop doesn't want to feel worried… Pop wants to enjoy the holiday.

What could Pop do to feel less worried? Think back to some of the calming exercises in this book and write your ideas here.

_____

_____

_____

_____

I AM A
GOOD FRIEND

PART 5: MAKE TIME FOR CALM

Find ways to feel calm every day. In this chapter we'll learn about relaxing and taking things slow.

ACTIVITY: FIND YOUR HAPPY PLACE

Your happy place is somewhere you feel calm, happy and safe. It might be somewhere you know very well, or somewhere from your imagination or memory.

Can you draw your happy place here?

When you want to feel calm, close your eyes and imagine being in your happy place.

Thinking of your happy place helps you to feel calm, but Pop is having trouble finding his – can you help Pop solve the maze?

ACTIVITY: FIVE SENSES CHECK-IN

Any time you'd like to feel calmer, you can check in with your senses, one by one. Take a deep breath and name:

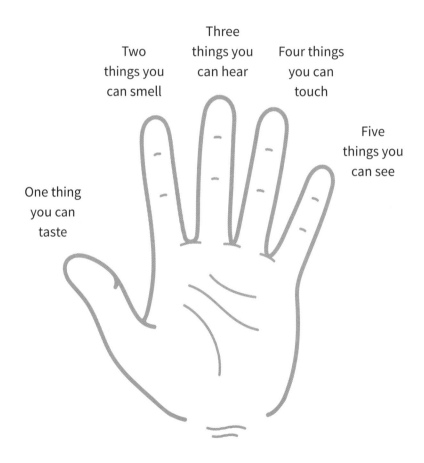

Three things you can hear

Two things you can smell

Four things you can touch

Five things you can see

One thing you can taste

How do you feel after checking in with your senses?

ACTIVITY: MINDFUL SCAVENGER HUNT

Make your five senses check-in into a game! You can play this by yourself or with friends. Grab a bag and find:

Something you can smell

Something you can see

Something you can touch

Something you can taste

Something you can hear

See who can collect everything on the list fastest!

ACTIVITY: GET CREATIVE

Imagine you're in a magical forest. What might you find there? Perhaps there are fantastical creatures, or delicious food growing from the trees! Use your favourite art materials to create a picture between the trees.

FINDING YOUR FLOW

When you're doing something that feels easy and fun, the sensation of peace you feel is called "flow". Everyone finds flow in different activities.

Painting   Building

Dancing   Drawing   Coding

Reading

Exploring   Singing

Writing

Inventing

Swimming

Learning

Gardening

Colouring

Running   Climbing

Sewing

Being with animals

Where do you find flow?

_____

_____

_____

_____

I CAN TAKE THINGS SLOW

ACTIVITY: DOODLING FOR CALM

Letting your pen and your mind wander is a great way to feel calm. Use the shapes below to start off your doodles!

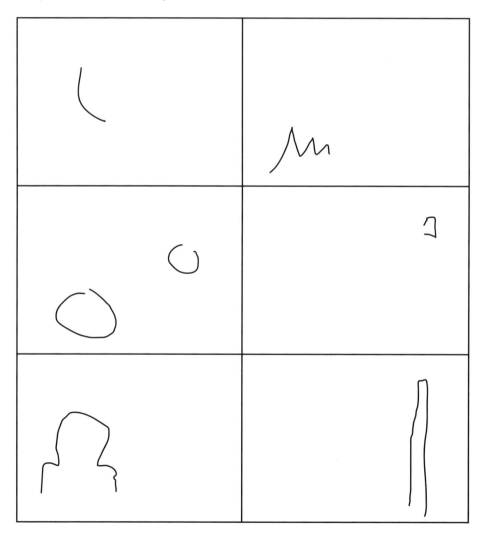

SWITCH OFF YOUR GADGETS

Gadgets are so much fun, but they're definitely not calming! Games and apps on tablets, computers and consoles are designed to make you feel excited, so when it's time to relax, turn off your gadgets. This is even more important when it's time to get ready for bed, because the light from a screen tricks your brain into being wide awake, so it's harder to get to sleep.

What are your favourite screen-free ways to relax? Write or draw them here.

ACTIVITY: SNAIL MAIL

Have you ever written a letter to a friend or family member? Writing letters is a brilliant calming activity, and a great way to show someone that you care. Plus, you might even get a letter back from them.

Here are some ideas for what to put in your letter:

🦋 Interesting things that have happened to you lately

🦋 Things you'd love to do but haven't yet

🦋 Dreams you've had

🦋 What your pets have been doing

🦋 Tricky things that have happened

🦋 What emotions you've been feeling

🦋 What you are planning to do in the next few weeks

🦋 Questions about the person you're writing to

Who will you write to?

THERE'S ONLY ONE ME!

ACTIVITY: POSITIVITY WORD SEARCH

Can you find the positive feelings in the word search?

E	A	H	Y	N	K	E	R	F	Q	O	H	G	S	D	A	B	X
O	I	H	S	M	Q	W	X	C	T	T	M	Z	A	D	R	S	D
F	D	S	E	R	I	Y	N	M	R	H	T	K	P	N	E	V	C
K	J	H	H	A	P	P	Y	U	K	G	F	S	A	C	L	N	S
F	C	A	E	N	M	J	Y	O	I	F	A	R	Y	I	A	O	D
Y	K	D	F	Z	X	X	C	V	D	G	L	P	E	R	X	H	S
R	D	G	F	H	I	U	K	J	N	F	G	R	Z	U	E	W	C
F	T	Y	J	K	S	X	C	E	V	C	A	V	J	D	D	S	V
S	R	V	J	N	Y	K	Y	U	K	O	S	X	V	J	S	A	D
D	R	D	O	V	D	S	E	M	H	N	U	K	E	F	B	W	I
R	A	Z	G	H	J	T	R	U	K	F	C	S	F	N	H	G	V
H	E	C	A	L	M	B	J	H	N	I	R	F	S	Z	W	D	S
E	F	S	D	G	U	H	V	A	K	D	E	J	A	J	N	Y	M
A	N	K	L	U	C	B	A	D	P	E	A	C	E	F	U	L	C
T	Y	X	K	S	K	R	D	J	S	N	J	X	K	W	I	H	S
A	H	D	C	A	R	A	B	S	K	T	E	U	C	A	K	E	J
U	D	V	Z	E	V	A	D	J	N	Y	W	D	V	D	A	Q
T	Y	U	N	S	W	E	D	V	S	W	H	K	B	X	E	F	E

Happy   Confident   Relaxed
Calm   Peaceful   Brave

ACTIVITY: TIME TO STRETCH

Stretching makes your body and mind feel calmer and more awake. Try these stretches whenever you need a boost.

Long like a snake:
Lie down on the floor, point your fingers and toes, and have a full body stretch.

Twist like a corkscrew:
Lie on your back and bend your knees; stretch your arms out to the sides. Lower your knees to the floor and look the opposite way, then swap sides.

Curled up like a cat:
Sit on your feet and stretch your arms along the floor in front of you.

Flutter like a butterfly:
Sit on your bottom and put the soles of your feet together. Flutter your knees up and down.

Tall like a cactus:
Stand tall and hold your arms out wide. Bend your elbows so your hands are pointing upward.

CALMING TOOLKIT

We've learned so many great ways to relax and feel calm in this chapter!
Which ones work for you? Draw a circle around your favourites:

Being creative

**Screen-free
activities**

**Five senses
check-in**

Doodling

**Imagining my
happy place**

Flow activities

Stretches

Writing a letter

I CAN GO WITH THE FLOW

PART 6: TAKING CARE OF YOURSELF

Taking good care of yourself will help you understand your emotions and feel good. In this chapter we'll learn about lots of different ways to look after your body and mind.

ACTIVITY: WHEN DO I FEEL MY BEST AND NOT SO GOOD?

It might be a place, a person or an activity that makes you feel your best. Think about where you are, who you're with and what you're doing when you feel calmest and happiest.

Write one or more ideas here:

_____

_____

_____

_____

_____

_____

_____

_____

_____

_____

_____

_____

_____

_____

_____

_____

_____

_____

_____

_____

_____

Think about what makes you feel worried, down or just not quite right. Perhaps there are certain people, places or activities that bring you these feelings.

Write one or more ideas here:

_____

_____

_____

_____

_____

_____

_____

_____

_____

_____

_____

Who or what could help you feel better?

_____

_____

_____

_____

_____

_____

_____

_____

_____

_____

_____

_____

ACTIVITY: I AM BRILLIANT

Use the space to draw a picture of yourself feeling brilliant. Think about what clothes you feel comfiest in and what activity you might be doing.

I'm feeling…_____

I'm with…_____

I'm doing…_____

HOW TO BE YOUR OWN BEST FRIEND

It might sound strange to say you can be your own best friend, but it's true! Even if you have a best friend already, you can still show yourself the same kindness, fun and generosity that best friends show each other.

Here's how:

- ❊ Spend time alone

- ❊ Listen to your body

- ❊ Be patient with yourself

- ❊ Use kind self-talk

- ❊ Do things you enjoy

- ❊ Say no with confidence

- ❊ Say yes with enthusiasm

- ❊ Ask for help when you need it

- ❊ Get plenty of sleep

- ❊ Eat healthily

- ❊ Drink plenty of water

- ❊ Move your body

I CAN DO
MY BEST

ACTIVITY: GRATITUDE JOURNAL

Gratitude means feeling thankful and noticing all the reasons you're lucky to be you. Keeping a journal of things you're grateful for each day helps you to feel more positive and less worried.

Use the spaces to keep a gratitude journal for one week. There's an extra idea each day to get you thinking.

Monday

I'm grateful for…

1._____

2._____

3._____

I'm proud because…_____

Tuesday

I'm grateful for…

1._____

2._____

3._____

I'm lucky because…_____

Wednesday

I'm grateful for…

1._____

2._____

3._____

I was brave when…_____

Thursday

I'm grateful for…

1._____

2._____

3._____

I felt good when…_____

Friday

I'm grateful for…

1._____

2._____

3._____

I was kind when…_____

Saturday

I'm grateful for…

1._____

2._____

3._____

It was funny when…_____

Sunday

I'm grateful for…

1._____

2._____

3._____

I felt calm when…_____

If you enjoyed keeping a gratitude journal, you can use any notebook or diary to carry on.

SLEEP CHART

How do you fall asleep at night? You might find it easy or hard – lots of young people need a bit of help from a grown-up, special blanket or teddy to get ready for sleep.

Write your bedtime routine here:

_____
_____
_____
_____

What are your favourite books for bedtime?

_____
_____
_____
_____

Do you brush your teeth first, or get in your pyjamas?

_____
_____
_____
_____

Do you have anything special in your bed that helps you sleep?

_____
_____
_____
_____

If you find it difficult to fall asleep, or you feel like you don't get enough sleep, it can have a big effect on your emotions. When we get plenty of rest, we feel calmer and more in control. When we're tired, it's much easier for big emotions to take over.

Try filling in this sleep chart every day, for a week, to see how sleep affects your feelings.

	Waking up was...	In the day I felt...	Going to sleep was...
Example	Tricky – I wanted to stay asleep	Hungry and grumpy	Easy – I felt very tired
Monday			
Tuesday			
Wednesday			
Thursday			
Friday			
Saturday			
Sunday			

ACTIVITY: EXERCISE

Exercise makes your mind and body feel great! Draw yourself doing your favourite kind of exercise here:

Cycling	Paddleboarding	Ice skating
Swimming		Playing outside
Dancing		Skateboarding
Running		Rock climbing
Climbing trees		Surfing
Football		Sailing
Walking		Scooting
Yoga	Trampolining	Basketball

EATING HEALTHILY

Eating plenty of healthy food means that your body can work properly – and your mind, too! Just like sleep, if your body hasn't had enough healthy food, it's more difficult to feel calm.

Every day, make sure you get a bit of every one of the main food groups:

 Carbohydrates to give you energy

 Protein to help your body grow

 Fats to store energy for later

Fruit and vegetables to help your digestive system

> **A few treats like sweets and cakes are OK, too! Food is for enjoying, as well as keeping your body healthy.**

ACTIVITY: DESIGN A HEALTHY MENU

You are hosting a grand feast! Your guests are hungry for yummy, healthy food. Can you come up with lots of delicious ideas for what you could all eat?

   Use your imagination to invent meals you'd love and be sure to include all the food groups!

THE HEALTHY MONSTER RESTAURANT

STARTERS

_____

_____

MAINS

_____

_____

SIDES

_____

_____

DESSERTS

_____

_____

DRINKS

_____

_____

I CAN LISTEN TO MY BODY

PART 7:
CELEBRATE YOURSELF

You've reached the final chapter of the book – well done! To finish up, you'll be thinking about all the ways in which you can use what you've learned to feel great about yourself every day.

MY FEELINGS GOLDEN RULES

You've learned so much about feelings! These are the golden rules to remember.

All feelings are OK

You are brilliant exactly as you are

You are allowed to express your feelings

Other people are alllowed to feel difficult feelings

The more you take good care of yourself, the better you'll feel

STORIES OF BIG FEELINGS

Joe, 9

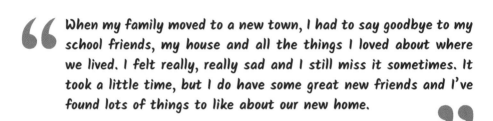

When my family moved to a new town, I had to say goodbye to my school friends, my house and all the things I loved about where we lived. I felt really, really sad and I still miss it sometimes. It took a little time, but I do have some great new friends and I've found lots of things to like about our new home.

Molly, 10

I've always loved gymnastics and when I was eight, I started doing competitions. I don't like the competitions as much as just learning and practising, and last summer there was a big competition. I got so nervous about it that I was having trouble sleeping and couldn't think about anything else. I felt scared to say I didn't want to do the competition, because my coach was counting on me, but I told my mum and she helped me tell my coach. It was such a relief to know I didn't have to go through with it, and I feel so much better now that I know I can always say "no".

Lily, 7

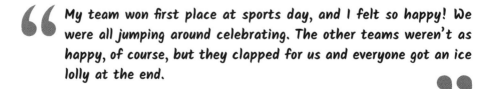

My team won first place at sports day, and I felt so happy! We were all jumping around celebrating. The other teams weren't as happy, of course, but they clapped for us and everyone got an ice lolly at the end.

Lucas, 11

 A few kids from the year above started teasing me one lunchtime. Everyone told me to just ignore them but when they started saying things about the colour of my skin, I felt so angry. I told them they were being racist and to leave me alone, and then I told my teacher about it. I'm really glad I stood up for myself and expressed my anger.

Jamie, 8

 When my Grandad died, it was really sad. All the grown-ups were sad, too, and I miss going to his house and playing in his garden. We had a funeral so we could all feel sad together and remember Grandad.

Erin, 10

 I once called the teacher "Mum" by accident. I can still feel my cheeks turning red just thinking about it – it was so embarrassing. Not many people noticed, and the teacher pretended it hadn't happened, but I still felt like I wanted to disappear. Argh! I'm sure it happened to someone else in my class last year, but I can't remember who it was.

MY FEELINGS EVERY DAY

You will always have feelings. If you never felt sad, you would not be able to feel happiness, so even though some emotions can be tricky, they're part of what makes life interesting and fun.

Every day, you can take care of your feelings in lots of different ways. For example, you could keep a diary – all it takes is a few minutes of thinking, and writing about your day and how you feel. You don't need any fancy equipment: any notebook can be a diary.

Give it a try – think about what has happened today and how you have felt, then write it here.

_____

_____

_____

_____

_____

_____

_____

_____

_____

_____

_____

_____

_____

_____

What would it be like to write in a diary every day for a year?

The end

You've reached the end of the book! Pop has enjoyed learning about feelings and how to take care of them – have you?

You can open up this book any time you like – to understand your own feelings, find a way to feel calm or help a friend to learn about emotions. You've done really well and you should feel very proud.

Remember: it's OK to be you, and your feelings are important.

MY FEELINGS MATTER

For parents and carers: How to help your child understand their feelings

Feelings are complicated for everyone. Even as an adult, they can feel confusing or overwhelming, and guiding your children through their emotions while looking after your own is quite the balancing act. The good news is, you don't need to be perfect or have it all worked out in order to support your child (and let's face it, none of us have it all worked out!).

The best place to start is by showing an interest and letting your child know that their feelings matter to you. Take notice of their body language and try to guess how they're feeling, before asking them about it, without any pressure to change the emotion. Showing curiosity rather than concern toward your child's feelings is a good approach, and it will help to inspire the same inquisitive spirit in them, too.

While respecting your child's feelings is important, this doesn't mean you should change your plans, rules or boundaries because of their emotional response. Show them that you take their feelings into consideration by acknowledging those emotions, showing empathy and talking through how you make decisions. This helps to teach them that it's safe to feel difficult feelings, and how to show respect to themselves and others in disagreements.

When your child's having trouble with big feelings, you can help them to feel calm in lots of ways. There are plenty of books and resources to guide you, and I've included some on pages 139 and 140. Whichever techniques you use to support your child, do so with confidence – this shows them that you're in control and they can trust you to guide them through difficult times.

You can set a good example by being aware of your own feelings. For example, if you're having a disagreement with your child and you feel yourself getting angry, say so – name the emotion and what you're going to do to help process it. You could say something like:

"I can feel myself getting angry so I'm going to take a few deep breaths in the kitchen – I'll be right back."

The more you talk about emotions, the more normal it will feel for your child, and the more they will understand and feel comfortable with their own and other people's feelings.

I hope you and your child find this book helpful. Emotions can be such a tricky subject and it's so upsetting to see a child struggling with theirs. Knowledge is power when it comes to feelings, and you're doing a great job by encouraging emotional intelligence early.

Further advice

If you're concerned about your child's emotional well-being, do talk it through with your GP. While almost all children experience intense feelings, some may need extra support. There are lots of great resources out there for information and guidance on children's mental health. Here are just a few:

Mind (UK)
www.mind.org.uk
0300 123 3393
info@mind.org.uk

BBC Bitesize (UK)
www.bbc.co.uk/bitesize/support

Childline (UK)
www.childline.org.uk
0800 1111

Child Mind Institute (USA)
www.childmind.org

The Youth Mental Health Project (USA)
www.ymhproject.org

Recommended reading

For children:
The Heart and the Bottle by Oliver Jeffers
HarperCollins, 2010

Happy, Healthy Minds: A Children's Guide to Emotional Wellbeing by The School of Life
The School of Life Press, 2020

For adults:
The Book You Wish Your Parents Had Read (and Your Children Will Be Glad That You Did) by Philippa Perry
Penguin, 2019

The Whole-Brain Child: 12 Proven Strategies to Nurture Your Child's Developing Mind by Dr Daniel J. Siegel and Dr Tina Payne Bryson
Robinson, 2012

Credits

pp.12, 13, 20, 21, 29, 31, 32, 36, 37, 41, 49, 50, 57, 62, 65, 69, 70, 76, 78, 79, 83, 86, 87, 95, 97, 99, 115, 119, 121, 130, 135 – monsters © mers1na/Shutterstock. com; p.13, 17, 23, 25, 54 – emoticons © SpicyTruffel/shutterstock.com; pp.18, 27, 28, 60, 80, 81 – shapes © VasiliyArt/shutterstock.com; pp.20, 25, 37, 41, 46, 57, 79, 86, 94, 95, 121 – bubbles © Paket/shutterstock.com; p.22 – rainbow © Gaston Bolivario/shutterstock.com; p.26 – brain © Blamb/shutterstock.com; p.31 – outline of child © Anna Rassadnikova/shutterstock.com; p.41 – pen © Puckung/shutterstock. com; p.41 – book © sinoptic/shutterstock.com; p.47 – mirror frame © Panda Vector/ shutterstock.com; p.49 – pen © IrynMerry/shutterstock.com p.49 – glasses © Intellson/ shutterstock.com; p.49 – notepad © sinoptic/shutterstock.com; p.57 – birthday present © Grommik/shutterstock.com; p.59 – sweet jars © Alex Ungureanu/shutterstock.com; p.59 – sweets © Alexandr III/shutterstock.com; p.66 – pause button © Albert999/ shutterstock.com; p.67 – snake © spiral media/shutterstock.com; p.68 – lion © spiral media/shutterstock.com; p.68 – bee © spiral media/shutterstock.com; p.69 – tree © nanmulti/shutterstock.com; p.70 – park © Aluna1/shutterstock.com; p.71 – colouring page © Elllyan/shutterstock.com; p.73 – lines © Alvaro Cabrera Jimenez/shutterstock. com; p.78 – cape © Rashad Ashur/shutterstock.com; p.83 – music notes © Martial Red/shutterstock.com; p.85 – shapes © wilkastok/shutterstock.com; p.87 – bubble © linear_design/shutterstock.com; pp.89, 90 – frames © theerakit/shutterstock.com; p.99 – maze © Venomous Vector/shutterstock.com; p.99 – beach © Alexandra Romanova/ shutterstock.com; p.100 – hand © Oleksandr Panasovskyi/shutterstock.com; p.101 – sweet © Alexandr III/shutterstock.com; p.101 – perfume bottle © olllikeballoon/ shutterstock.com; p.101 – bell © Visual Generation/shutterstock.com; p.101 – remote control © M. Adebadal/shutterstock.com; p.101 – book © Katerin_vin/shutterstock. com; pp.102, 103 – trees © ugarich/shutterstock.com; pp.111, 112 – yoga poses © redchocolate/shutterstock.com; p.115 – bubble bath © nadiia_oborska/shutterstock. com; p.119 – glass of water © Francois Poirier/shutterstock.com; p.119 – skipping rope ©hchjjl/shutterstock.com; p.127 – food © bioraven/shutterstock.com; p.130 – party hat, balloons © AnyaLis/shutterstock.com

Other books in the series...

£10.99
Paperback
ISBN: 978-1-78783-699-0

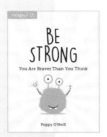

£10.99
Paperback
ISBN: 978-1-78783-607-5

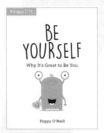

£10.99
Paperback
ISBN: 978-1-78783-608-2

£10.99
Paperback
ISBN: 978-1-78685-236-6

£10.99
Paperback
ISBN: 978-1-78685-235-9

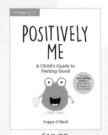

£10.99
Paperback
ISBN: 978-1-80007-169-8

Other Vie books for parents, carers and children...

£10.99
Paperback
ISBN: 978-1-80007-337-1

£10.99
Paperback
ISBN: 978-1-80007-168-1

£10.99
Paperback
ISBN: 978-1-78783-990-8

£10.99
Paperback
ISBN: 978-1-78783-537-5

My Healthy Mind Series for parents, carers and children...

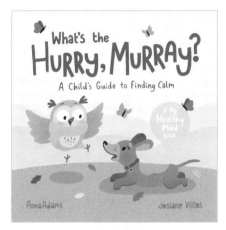

£6.99
Paperback
ISBN: 978-1-80007-016-5

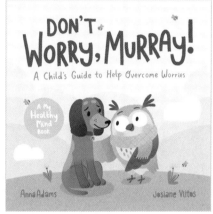

£6.99
Paperback
ISBN: 978-1-80007-015-8

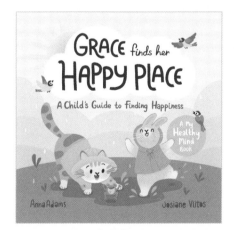

£6.99
Paperback
ISBN: 978-1-80007-017-2

£6.99
Paperback
ISBN: 978-1-80007-018-9

Have you enjoyed this book?
If so, why not write a review on your favourite website?

If you're interested in finding out more about our books,
find us on Facebook at **Summersdale Publishers**, on Twitter
at **@Summersdale** and on Instagram at **@summersdalebooks**
and get in touch. We'd love to hear from you!

Thanks very much for buying this Summersdale book.

www.summersdale.com